THE THINGS I DO KNOW

Developing the Mindset for Success

Todd Speciale

The Things I Do Know: Developing the Mindset of Success
Copyright © 2017 by Purpose Press

DEDICATION

To my wife, Michelle, who's stood by me in all the good and all the bad. You define loyalty in love, laughter and life and I thank you for never doubting the man you always knew I could be. To my, children, Averigh, Addyson and Abriella who have not only made me a better man, but taught me as much about life as I may ever teach you. You girls give me a reason to breathe and daddy will never stop knowing you're counting on me to be your hero.

To my mother, who's the strongest woman I know and believed in me even when I didn't. To my father, who's staring down from heaven above, I say to you; "Dad I did it. Just as you told me I could. I miss you more than life and today, know this is only the beginning of how I'm going to impact the world, making you proud."

To my brother, Robert Speciale and his beautiful family Kim, Krista and Tristan. There were days when I wanted to give up and questioned my ability to be more. Without your help, every single step of the way, this wouldn't have been possible. A simple thank you, just doesn't seem enough. I'm so grateful for you.

To the Minors, my amazing in-laws, I owe so much of my success to you pushing me to be all I can be. Art, Karen and Nick, I'm stronger and more dedicated to achieving great things with you by my side. For that, I'm forever in your debt.

Thank you, my entire family, for allowing me to follow my passion, make my dreams become a reality and prove to others they can too.

TABLE OF CONTENTS

INTRODUCTION

I know you. You have the desire to do greater, to be better, to see more than what you see in front of you. Life's situations and circumstances often make it difficult for you to get to the vision you have for yourself. You ask yourself, "Who am I to do these amazing things? Am I even capable or qualified? I don't even know where to begin doing the things I dream of doing."

Well, I'm here to tell you that you can and will achieve those great things. I know because I was once you, asking the same questions and having the same doubts. It happened for me and it can and will for you too, but it will not happen if you don't believe in yourself first.

When you begin to adopt habits of highly successful people and begin to truly believe in the power you harness, you will start to see the various areas of your life explode with success. I didn't believe in myself or the power I had to help transform lives; mine or others. I didn't realize that everything I needed was already within me, I just had to discover it and prepare myself to put the work in so I could be used effectively in showing people how to harness their best selves.

My success did not come overnight. It didn't come without hard work and perseverance. It didn't come without days where I asked myself, "What am I doing? Can I really do this?" I understand the questions that dance in your head. I know what negative thoughts you may be entertaining. I also know that once you decide to turn all of that off, you'll never regret it.

I had to come to some hard truths within myself years ago, and my daughters helped me to realize those truths. You see, sometimes you will have people cross your path that will help you realize that you're just sitting on your gifts and talents. Sometimes they will tell you gently. Sometimes it will be a harsh wakeup call for you. I'm not here to tell you gently. I'm here to be your wake-up call. I'm here to shake you and show you just how powerful you are. I need you to see just how many lives you can help transform once you become aware of the powerhouse that you are.

Within these pages, you will find the very things I had to learn to be able to come to those realizations on my own. Within these pages, you will find the words to help you walk in the talents and gifts you are already equipped with. Within these pages, you will find the things I do know about personal success, what it takes to achieve it, and the various lessons I've learned. My job is to push you, to awaken you, so you realize that you are already more than enough for everything you need and want in life.

"Chains of habit are too light to be felt, until they are too heavy to be broke."

Warren Buffet

HABIT

Habits are why we don't succeed. If you don't learn to control your thoughts, you will never be able to control your behavior.

Habit is defined as a settled or regular tendency or practice, especially one that is hard to give up. If this doesn't say it all, I don't know what does.

Here's what I do know:

I know that I used to allow myself to let "habit" take over my life. Think about this from every angle. For instance, how about fitness? How many times have you said you were going to start Monday and never did? Then something inevitably happens. An event, dinner with the in-laws or just driving by a fast food joint and you say to yourself, "One more day won't kill me."

How about the times you start to work out and start out all pumped and ready to crush it? You go super hardcore, buy new workout clothes, buy all the equipment you think you'll need, join a gym and then after a few weeks two things happen. You either feel great and continue to crush, or you slowly fall back and make excuses as to why you'll catch up to your routine tomorrow. As time passes, it's like a stretched rubber band that continues to go back to its original position, and you find yourself back at square one again.

This is all habit, believe it or not. When you are used to living a certain way of life, you have to be ready to change your process consciously. Your mindset has to be in an exact state where you only see the end goal. You have to stay focused and truly believe you can make a positive difference in your life.

When you start to tell yourself you need to work out, then you're lying in bed one night and get that sweet tooth craving. You get up to grab some candy and the next thing you know you're 2000 calories deep right before bedtime selling yourself on why eating this junk is ok. This is habit. You are used to eating what you want, when you want. It takes willpower and pure strength to overcome and get yourself on the right track; which the strong do and so can you!

Now let's talk about habit from a life or business standpoint. How many times have you had a great idea and decided to get together with another great mind to make this idea come to life? As an entrepreneur, I know it happens multiple times, only to see the realization that without massive action, your dream cannot become a reality. It slowly fades out.

It then becomes just another memory of a great idea that never came to fruition. There's no secret. A new idea, a new business, a new goal, a new life all takes hard work, determination and the will to succeed beyond what you truly think it takes to become successful.

Now, how many of us have started that idea, bought the corporation documents, formed and organized the individuals to run the company, and actually gone out and sought business? Unfortunately, due to your everyday job, you allowed your great plan to fall off, or you blame "lack of time" to the destruction of a massive master plan to take over an industry?

Look, many of you right now are thinking of ideas you once had. You're saying to yourself, "Damn he's right, that's me!" Well, guess what? It was me too. I've had that great idea and expected huge things to happen, but then habit hit me. HABIT defines our lives in more ways than we'd like to think.

Is motivation, dedication, education, the will to win, and courage all contributing factors to success? Of course, but not without training yourself to allow good habits to truly alter the way you do things, and the belief in your soul that life can be better. By deciding today that your habit is going to change into a positive form of utilizing massive action as your ability to overcome the mass mindset of mediocrity, only then can you guarantee yourself to be that much closer to your dreams and victory of the life you want to live!

Habit can either keep you down or take you to places you've only dreamt. Habit does not have to be only negative. Too many of us associate habit with things like smoking and addiction in all forms rather than embracing what it is truly meant for. It's about creating a life where your mind is forced to grow through a positive form, taking massive action, guaranteeing huge results today, tomorrow and for years to come. This changes "habit" to a word that lifts us up rather than keeps us down!

Let's do this:

Right now, as we speak, write down one thing you've always wanted to accomplish. Something you've set out to do, started, but never finished because you let habit in a negative way take over.

You have the chance to be different right now. You have the opportunity to embrace change in a positive way and make your life different this very moment!

You have the opportunity to take your abilities to the next level by allowing your soul to produce the willpower to wake up every day, look yourself in the mirror and say, "today I refuse to let the negative form of anything take over my life. Today, I decide to be more, to feel more, to push my mind, body, and soul to guarantee that every dream becomes a reality. Today is the anniversary of my new life. I rose to every occasion and made damn sure nothing will ever beat me or bring me down.

I will form habits in every positive fashion to show the world the true meaning of that word, what it's meant for, and that there's greatness in what we all can accomplish!"

Read that a few times and then yell it out! Scream it! Turn on your favorite song and start to dance! Today is the first day of the rest of your life. Today we write down our goals and form the habit to shape our lives forever! So, before you move on to the next chapter, write down the challenging moments in your life where you allowed "habit" in its worst form to stop you from achieving something that could have been great.

Give yourself a timeline of when you want to accomplish those things you KNOW you can accomplish and make them your priority.

The best feeling ever is getting something done you once thought you couldn't. The opportunities after that point, are endless. You'll begin to imagine yourself doing

things some only dream of. That, people, is the moment
your life changes forever; through positive habit!

GOAL   **DATE ACHIEVED**

_____

_____

_____

_____

_____

_____

_____

_____

_____

_____

_____

_____

_____

_____

_____

_____

_____

_____

_____

_____

"Some people only hate you because of the way other people love you."

Anonymous

HATE

I'm not even sure where to start because this chapter was the one where I didn't want to go off the deep end. However, I get beyond upset at the levels and the great lengths people will go to ruin or sabotage a vision, a career, a belief, a dream, a family, or even a life. All of that over what? Is it bitterness, jealousy, self-confidence issues, low self-esteem, lack of growth, or is it because they're doing something you feel you can't?

I believe this world is growing worse and worse when it comes to the truth about wanting others to succeed.

Why can't we clap when others win? Why can't we smile when they accomplish a goal? Why can't we pat someone on the back for doing something that may be very small to us, but very big to them? Why do we question the ability of others to change the world? What good does it do to laugh at the efforts of those with passion in believing they can do more? Why is it necessary to tell others to be "realistic" in their thoughts? Why does society try to prove, today more than ever, that what you dare to dream just isn't possible?

I'm tired of this. I get sick to my stomach when I see the hate. It's getting worse and diluting the kindness of our children. Nowadays, bullying is worse than ever. We, as individuals laugh at the people who are unique, rather than see the light and the positivity of who they are. We trash the old, stay stagnant with the present, and see the future by chance rather than by determination and the will to believe there's more to what we all have to offer.

A great idea gets bombarded with excuses. We are told a goal isn't "realistic." Passion is just a dream. A dream is just a wish that we can't control.

All of these symptoms of society are drawn by hate or lack of power in themselves! This isn't about you. If you let people change your course than shame on you! This is your life, not theirs. The information we receive will resonate in our minds only if we want it to! It's called selective hearing. This is a real thing. It is the moment you decide that you don't have to listen to what everyone says.

Only listen to what your heart is telling you. What your mind says, you can forget. Whatever your passion is that makes your heart feel full, this is what represents you as a person, not the opinions of others.

People that hate don't realize the instability of their souls. There's so much they are missing that they could use within them to be more. Instead of lifting people up, they get a high off of trying to bring you down. I've said it too many times, when people say or do anything negative to or about others, it comes from a place of pure weakness. There's something that is lacking in them, and since they can't figure out what it is, they want to make sure they do what they can to keep others "at their level."

"Hate"- to dislike intensely or passionately; feel extreme aversion for or extreme hostility toward; detest.

"Hater" - a person simply cannot be happy for another person's success. Rather than be happy for someone, they make a point of trying to expose a flaw in that person.

These definitions are fact, but only if we allow them to affect us. We can either read into them and let them knock us off course, or simply use as fuel to do more. There's an old saying "the more haters you have, the more successful you are." Pile them up, people. As a matter of fact, take applications! Let them stand in line. Let them talk. Let them try and derail you. The moment you decide to fight back, but continue moving forward, is the moment you'll get to a level of greatness you've only imagined.

Here's what I do know:

If they weren't talking about you, then you wouldn't be doing anything right. You have to be changing lives, changing your own life, or going in the right direction if they're taking an interest in you. You can't expect for your life to be smooth sailing, but what you can do is take control of the people you let on your boat.

It all comes down to surrounding yourself with like-minded, successful people, who love to see you win. Have people who will stand beside you and fight the good fight. Who do you know who believes we can grow as one, rather than apart? Who do you know will lift you up when you feel like you have fallen? Who do you know will lend that hand when you need one to hold onto? These individuals are worth every second of your life.

Just remember, a hater's fuel comes from seeing you suffer, not succeed or proving what they say to be true when you don't persevere. Your job is to prove that if you're not flying, you're running. If you can't run, you'll walk. If you can't walk, you'll crawl. Whatever you can, you must always be moving towards your dream!

Be passionate about overcoming the negativity in your life. Embrace those who aren't as strong and do what you can to help strengthen them. If they aren't willing to change, remove them from your life for good. Life's too short to poison your mind with malicious content.

Your time on this earth is to show the world who you are and what you are made of. It won't be easy, but I believe in you. I guess the only question is.... do you believe in you?

Let's do this:

We know there are haters, and it probably won't take long for you to point out who they are in your life. But, take some time to identify the people in your life that are not haters. Who are the ones that support you? Who are the people that are in your corner? Who is it that wants you to succeed and live your dreams; they even push you toward them?

They may or may not be family so don't go with the easy answers. Pay attention to who has proven themselves with their positive actions. List as many people as you can and how they have shown that they want you to win. Make sure you keep them close and appreciate them.

_____

_____

_____

_____

_____

_____

_____

_____

_____

_____

"All glory comes from daring to begin."

Eugene F. Ware

START

It's not about yesterday. It's about today and what you're going to do to with the gift God has given you called NOW! Don't take for granted the days we have, the minutes we have, even the seconds we have! Yes, we have to live life optimistically, but let's put things into perspective real quick.

God forbid, but let's say that a doctor told you right now that you had four months left to live. What would you do? How would you live? Where would you go? How would you spend your time? Would you be afraid to do things you once were?

Read this sentence out loud. "I would choose to LIVE from the second I heard that I might not live." Does that make any sense? To some maybe, but to me, it absolutely does not. See, the mindset behind waiting to do what you're afraid of, what you're scared to do, worrying about how others might perceive you or just simply deciding not to do something you've always wanted to do and just pushing it off is called PROCRASTINATION. It is based on a belief that tomorrow is promised. Well, guess what? It's not.

Here's what I do know:

We all have that clock. We don't know when it's going to run out so we have to live every day as if there were no tomorrow.

Love unconditionally. Be loyal to the people that are loyal to you. Smile at everyone you see. Promote happiness. Give. Learn as much as you can. Lift people up. Be thankful for what you have at this very moment. Find the good in today and now. Whatever higher power you believe in, thank them for today. Take today by storm. Guarantee growth. Change a life. Most importantly have faith that you're exactly where you need to be at this very moment.

Many of you have a hard time finding the good that we're blessed with in times of struggle. Are we going to have challenging days, days of loss, days that test our faith, days that seem like nothing goes right? Absolutely! These days are there to train us to be stronger than we thought we could be.

Let me ask you this: Are you "that person" that says, "It just never ends." "I can't get a break." "Nothing goes my way." "Life sucks." "Why is this happening to me?" "I don't deserve this." "Is anything ever going to go my way?" Now think.

Truly think about how your life is. Do you have friends that love you? Family that loves you? A roof over your head? Food on the table? A job? Clothes on your back? Healthy children? A healthy spouse? Are you healthy? And what I mean by healthy is alive and well! Do you have a car? Do you have a TV? How about air conditioning? Should I go on?

Look, if I'm being honest, Im so sick and tired of the "woe is me" attitude in the world. If you've said yes to any of the above, you don't realize how blessed you are Do you realize that your higher power has allowed you to live? Do you know every tiny moment in your life has guided you to the exact point where you are right now as you read this?

I can't stand how society decides to program our minds to concentrate on the few "trying times" rather than concentrating on all the good that's in your life. This mindset destroys dreams.

I'll tell you a quick story. When I was at my worst, I sat in a dark room in which I paid to have my windows tinted so no light would come in, watching TV all day, depressed because I couldn't afford gas to drive from one end of town to the next to see my daughters after their mother and I split up.

I used to cry for hours at a time every day and yell out "why is this happening to me?" I used to find every excuse and someone to blame for my current circumstances. I used to lie to myself until I actually believed what I was saying was true. As a matter of fact, I even made a list of all the "trying times" that had happened in my life just to prove to myself I was cursed. In my head, I was doomed and meant to be a failure.

When my daughters would come see me, I was living with two roommates in a house where we used to run poker games for a living. I thought my time with them wasn't that exciting. I had no money to take them places and we ate ramen noodles many days. Then one day, I realized I had to make a change.

I was clinically depressed. They came to me in the morning, and I couldn't get out of bed to spend time with them. I was so depressed my body didn't function. All I wanted to do was lay in bed, close my eyes, and hope that I never woke up. To me, my life couldn't get any worse. All I was doing was concentrating on all the rough things in my life and felt like the world was coming down on me. The truth is, my perception of my world couldn't be more wrong.

That day, I remember lying in bed, hearing my kids laughing and playing with my roommate and it didn't matter to me. I had been in the worst state of mind. I figured I'll play with them tomorrow. My roommate was up all day with them. He took them to get food with his own money. They went to the park, then came home and had some play sand, letting my girls make a mess all over the kitchen table. He kept them happy. He spent quality time with them, and all I could do was sleep. When I woke up, it was 8pm and they were sitting in the living room. I had missed all these moments with them, and it just didn't matter to me.

About 20 mins after I woke up, their mother picked them up and I wouldn't see them for another three days as we had split time. I couldn't wait to go back to bed. I took for granted the blessings that were right in front of my eyes. The laughter. The smiles. The love. The health of my girls. My health. The time I had with them. The roof over our heads. The food. The growth in watching them live life before me.

My mind was in such a bad place that I couldn't focus on the good. I could only see all the bad in my life. This mindset crushes people. It demolishes any chance of hope or faith and only you can change that. There is no one in the world that can change you, except you! You have to program your mind to see all that you are fortunate to have every day. Concentrate on committing yourself to being thankful for everything you have, every day.

So, one day I woke up and saw a text message from my oldest daughter, Averigh. She said, "Daddy, I know you're tired a lot, but Addyson and I really want to spend time with you when we come over." I replied, "Of course baby." She said, "Are you sure daddy? Because you said that before and you go back to sleep." I sat there for a minute realizing that I have taken for granted the time I've been given with the blessings that have been given to me.

I replied, "Baby, daddy loves you and I'm sorry. I will try." But then I read that text message and couldn't believe I replied "I'll try." How dare I? What was I thinking? These are my girls. They're supposed to be the reason I get up, not the reason I lay down. My daughter replied, "It's ok daddy. We know you're tired. We love you, and our time together, we just hope you love it too."

At this point, reading that reply from my daughter, broke me down. It hit home harder than anything ever had. My own daughter, 8 years old, had just sent me a message wondering if I cared. Wondering If I loved my time with them. Questioning me wanting to be with them. I started crying uncontrollably and started screaming "Why me?!" I was yelling at God, asking "Why are you doing this to me? Why can't my life be good?"

Then it hit me. There was about a thirty-second pause. I was breathing hard, trying to calm myself down. I looked over on my nightstand and saw the list of all the so-called "bad" in my life. I grabbed it and started writing a list of all the good. Then another one of everything I've been taking for granted. I was shocked at all the good things outweighing the bad, and even more shocked at the things I've been taking for granted knowing that tomorrow isn't promised.

I started thinking about how my girls would see me. Who would they say their father is if I continued to lay down and not fight? What type of legacy would I leave for them? How would they speak of me to others? Would they even know they're my world? What type of example am I setting for them if I'm ignoring the blessings right before my eyes?

Am I sending a message to just give up when life gets hard? Is it ok to take for granted the good things in life? The questions started flowing as I continued to write out all of the good things in my life. I couldn't stop. I started remembering who I am. My energy started to rebuild. I was getting excited! I couldn't believe how I was ignoring the opportunities and gifts I'd been given. I screamed at the top of my lungs, "No more!"

That day changed my life forever. My mindset was different from the second I compared the so-called "bad things" in my life to the good things in my life, realizing what I had taken for granted. The truth is, we all have that turning point. We just need to recognize it for ourselves.

I owe my life to my daughters. They proved to me that no matter how rough it gets; they were still there. They are healthy. They are smiling. They didn't need or want anything other than to spend time with daddy. They saved me!

The moral of this story is to recognize, embrace, and be thankful for the good that's in your life. No matter how rough life gets, just step back take a breath and look around you. See the gifts that you've been given, even if it's a loaf of bread in the fridge. Knowing you won't go hungry is a blessing. But more importantly, know that every "negative" situation has a positive, but it's up to you to find it. It's up to you not to allow your situation to dictate your future.

Let's do this:

Write out all the positives in your life. Challenge yourself to look beyond the easy to identify things like just listing family, a job, a place to live, and other general things. Get specifics. Look at the things we take for granted every day. From the ability to put on our shoes by ourselves to the freedoms we neglect daily. Write as much as you need and look back at it regularly so you remember to be grateful.

_____

_____

_____

_____

_____

"You cannot have a positive life with a negative mind."

Joyce Meyer

ENERGY

It all starts with energy! It's funny how so many people get up short-winded, stagnant, and lazy with no want or need to produce positive energy daily. I can't understand it. I have people asking me how I do it. Simply put, life is about the ability to grow while allowing your mind to flourish through a set of emotions that gets you to the place you want to be.

We're all different. We can't be someone, or something we're not, but what we can do is strive to be more in a way that only proves to ourselves who we are individually.

Energy starts from the minute your eyes open. From the first breath you take. From the first movement of getting out of bed. It shapes your entire day. If you wake up unready and not willing to give 100%, you'll never give 100%. You have to be strong and realize that you have something so special about who you are and need to share it with the world in a fashion that will attract people to you.

Many of us see the energy as affecting our souls personally, and it does, but what we don't realize is that we touch every life we're around. Our actions determine the way we reach those in our path. You have to wake up knowing there's so much more to life than just you. I'm shaking my head writing this, because it bothers me that people can go through a day, negatively affecting someone's life and close their eyes peacefully as they lay their head down at night. This is all due to the energy you give off.

It's astonishing to see what a strong presence of energy can do in the morning. It's amazing to see when you feel someone isn't participating, or to see what eye contact can do when they realize the energy connecting one person to the next can change their entire persona.

Motivation and lifting others up all stems from the energy you possess and the energy you give to those you surrounded. You cannot expect positive vibes to have growth in your co-workers when you aren't doing anything to guarantee or help the future as a whole.

Outstanding success in people willing to expand their horizons is gained when a true leader shows what can and will be done with the right amount of energy and mindset. Do you want to be on top? Work harder. Do you want to change a life? Pull someone aside and do what it takes to make them better.

Here's what I do know:

You can't allow a bad day to change you. You can't allow those with negative mindsets to alter your path. You can't allow a personal problem, financial problem or even a health issue to change your energy. You have to find the constant ability to maintain a mindset and energy balance to see the good in what you have, not only in your life but what you have to offer the world as a whole.

The stamp you leave today will forever be known as your legacy. What type of legacy do you want to leave? What example do you want to set for your children? What type of atmosphere do you present for the ones who look up to you in all aspects of your life? These are all questions that have to be answered.

It blows my mind that some go to work hating what they do. Do you think that energy resonates well with others? Do you think the aura you present to the world lifts you up or lifts up those around you? Don't be selfish. Yes, we all have problems, but problems can be a good thing. It's all about how you see them. You can find the good in all situations by breaking down the value each will add to your life.

If life were all sunshine and rainbows, there would never be growth. There would never be success giants that came from nothing. Stop kidding yourselves. The rich haven't always been rich. It wasn't a magic wand that shifted their lives from poverty to superstardom. It was massive action! Massive energy! Massive willpower! Every moment you let a negative mindset in is a moment you've lost that could have changed your life forever.

What if you woke up, looked in the mirror and said, "Here's what I do know." I know that if I don't work hard to reach my goals, I may not be able to give my loved ones the life they deserve. I may not be able to prove to myself, and the world, who I am as a person. I may not be able to lead by example, not just as a professional, but as a mentor and example for my children as well. I may not be able to pass along the energy that's needed to those I come in contact with, to maximize my day and show the world all I have to give.

Now what if you say, "I also know…" I know that the moment I give the energy I know I can, it'll not only affect the energy in those around me, but also guarantee ultimate results in growth. Smiling, laughing, not having to force the positive energy in the work environment, or in your personal lives and simply being thankful to breathe, and being able to come home to those you love most should be the daily goal. It sounds hard, right? It's really not.

We've all been in difficult circumstances. We've been in positions that test our well-being as humans, and we either stand up and fight or get knocked down. The energy deep within your soul is the game changer. For instance, my father was very sick and in the hospital around May of 2017. He has several things that aren't going his way. He has been in and out of the hospital for about two years, and more than once they told us, "Prepare for the worst. He may not have a lot of time left." Being the typical old-school tough Italian man he is, he just defied the odds and continued to fight back, winning at every moment they said he couldn't. He's always been the type of guy who doesn't give up. This is a prime example of how energy transfers from father to son and becomes drastically influential in times of triumph.

Early May, my father fell and hit his head on the bed pretty hard. He was knocked unconscious, and we called the ambulance. They came and got him, only to realize once hospitalized, that he had perforated an artery in his skull and blood is leaking into his brain cavity. At 85 years old, he was as fragile as can be. They didn't have any other choice but to operate and remove the leaking blood or, due to the hemorrhaging, he wouldn't last more than a few days. They scheduled him for surgery in just a few hours and warned us that he might not make it through.

Guess what? He did! He fought through, and although he ended up with 17 staples in his skull, he came out happy to be alive. We were all praying and using every bit of energy we had to keep him on the right track, and it worked!

Unfortunately, my father started declining after the surgery. They found out he had also had a minor stroke during his fall, and that it affected not only his brain activity but his motor function too. We would learn that his overall motor functions would start to diminish as the days go on. He couldn't swallow anymore, so they had to feed him intravenously. He couldn't speak, and could barely keep his eyes open. As strong as my dad was, we kept the faith that he would soon recover as he had many times in the past.

Late that month, I got a phone call conferencing in the nurse practitioner and the doctor that's oversaw my father's activity while admitted. They stated that if he continued to decline, being non-responsive, that he would have only about 4-5 weeks left to live.

During this time, my job was to motivate sales individuals daily. Keeping people happy, pumped up, and doing what I could to guarantee growth and maximum success for my company. That was my goal. But, I kept having these thoughts of losing my hero.

This was one of the hardest things I'd ever dealt with. The truth is, my father would want me to go on spreading positive energy and changing every life I touch. He wouldn't want me suffering through his sickness, passing that sorrow on to others. I remembered him telling me time and time again growing up, "It's about what you do for others that will define you as a man." That day I stayed positive, put on a smile and continued to lift everyone up.

After I left work that day, I broke down in tears sitting in my car in the parking lot. It was finally time for me to let go. I had to realize that things weren't looking up for my father. I couldn't hold it in anymore knowing he was suffering. It's times like this that challenge us. These moments force us to make choices that directly affect our future. That evening I went home, cried to my wife and fell asleep praying for my father's speedy recovery.

The next morning, I woke up and had a choice to make. I could either lay in bed upset at what the future may hold for my father and those who love him, or I could get up and push through using every ounce of energy I had to show the world that even in the toughest of times we can find the will to persevere.

That day, many people came up to me and asking me how I was doing it. They continued to say if the tables were turned, or if it were them, they wouldn't be strong enough to do what I was doing. My answer to them was simple. The second you realize the value and impact you have on the lives around you, is the moment you become responsible for being the best person you can be. Thus, allowing the transfer of positive energy to fulfill the lives of all who depend on you daily.

The moral of this story is to understand that energy, defined as "the strength and vitality required for sustained physical or mental activity," only stems from the will to be the best version of yourselves with no exception to this rule. You can't expect the best from all and only do half your part. Karma is energy. Treat others the way you'd like to be treated. Wouldn't this world be a better place if we all promoted energy as a positive way of lifting each other up, not only when needed, but just because it's the right thing to do?

You want people to look at you and say, "Where do you get all that energy from? How do you stay so positive?" The simple answer is making others realize their potential in changing the world in a great way daily through the energy they put off, is well within their reach. That is exactly how we start to win.

Just remember, as there are multiple forms of energy, deep within, the most powerful energy is what comes from your heart, your will, your desire to make the world a better place. There's just no excuse for anything less. Live by this rule and not only will you impact every life you touch, but you'll start to grow to levels beyond your wildest dreams.

Reserve your energy for your highest and best use. Guarantee that when you set in stone that the ONLY way you're going to live your days is by passing along positive energy, then and only then will you finally be ready to surpass your biggest goals. This my friends, is essential to a society of exponential growth.

Let's do this:

Take a few moments to write down at least three ways you can give positive energy to others each day. Make them unique to you, your style, and your personality. It could be leaving little notes to a spouse, counting the number of strangers you smile at each day, or doing a random act of kindness. DO NOT list things you already do. Tap into your creative energy.

_____

_____

_____

_____

_____

_____

_____

_____

_____

_____

"Success is a measure decided by others. Satisfaction is a measure as decided by you."

Anonymous

GRATIFICATION

When you delay instant gratification, you will experience long-term satisfaction. Gratification is defined as pleasure, especially when gained from the satisfaction of a desire or accomplishment. When we talk about this word, its definition seems to be so broad and open to interpretation. The explanation is the same, but the outcome in its satisfaction seems to be a wider range than most think.

Maxwell Maltz said, "The ability to discipline yourself to delay gratification in the short term in order to enjoy the greater rewards in the long term, is the indispensable prerequisite for success." He just nailed it! Too many of us need to feel instant gratification in life to feel the immediate effect of accomplishing something in our lives. We think too short term, there are absolutely no shortcuts to any place worth going.

The minute we get past the materialistic superficial wants or needs we feel we must have to engage in instant gratification, we begin to connect deeper to our souls, as well as to those around us. We can then see a more fulfilled long-term effect of succession leaving a legacy of true self-worth, rather than short term luxuries. This process has proven to be crucial to the inner growth of the majority of industry giants leading our world to better places.

We all see gratification in different ways. If used properly, it can expand our minds to different levels of intellect. Some people pat themselves on the back for something personally accomplished, which is needed and worth doing if not taken advantage of. Some see a much higher purpose of helping others reach levels of exceptionalism that most may never see. The rule to live by is to smile when others win, but smile brighter when you've impacted that life to help them win.

Here's what I do know:

This world is falling into an epic hole of individuals concentrating on self-gratification on what they've personally accomplished, rather than lifting others up. It seems arrogance and cockiness has forced its way into the masses. What we fail to realize is there is a clear difference between confidence and arrogance. We can't allow our personal triumphs to overlook the ones trying to accomplish great things around us. This is going to cripple our economy and the minds of our children in having them think "it's all about them."

In professional speaking, they teach you to be very careful using the words "me" or "myself." This doesn't mean they can't be used, but they must be used in an engaging context where others can learn and benefit from your story. Too many of us have the wrong idea of what true happiness is. It's not attained through self-gratification, but instead through realizing your ability to affect the world, guaranteeing an impact to a higher purpose in life. The gratification comes in doing, not in the result.

Success takes hard work, dedication, patience, practice, and a complete understanding of self-awareness. Why do we feel the need for self-gratification? Simple. We want to know when we win. Just know this, the world sees you. The day you feel it necessary to be noticed, is the day you won't be. You have to have faith that when you are noticed, it will come from your abilities to thrive in your specific area of expertise and won't need to be forced. People are drawn to positive energy and good vibes, not arrogance and a need for entitlement.

I also know that people are usually willing to trade what they want at this very moment for what they want most. In today's world, everything seems to be that "now" factor. Trust me, instant gratification is overrated. It's about the process. It's the hard times. It's the fight and your ability to achieve things others won't. It's about moments, not just one moment. This is what makes life worth living, and the day you realize this, the delayed impact of your gratification will be like an awakening to your soul with love, life, and fulfillment like you've never felt before.

Never let the tough times you're going through compare to the joy you're going to feel from finding opportunity in what most see as a negative in their lives.

I'll end this chapter with this, you deserve to feel accomplished. You are entitled to smile when you win. You must love yourself. You must have confidence in your ability to overcome anything, and must be thankful you have the passion and intelligence to do just that.

You have the power to obtain massive wealth. You must be proud when you set a goal and reach it, but never, ever stop believing you can do more! You have greatness in you, but don't ever forget the greatness in the ones around you as well.

The most powerful gratification you will ever feel is positively impacting someone's life. Be that person! Let gratitude come to you, don't ask for it. Remember, mediocre people do exceptional things all the time! It's up to you how you define gratification in your life and how you want to utilize the power of it in your life. Never take for granted the effect your personal gratification can have on others. Lift others up with it and watch how quickly the world changes in a positive way. Today we begin.

Let's do this:

Think of moments that are personally gratifying to you. Write those down first. They may include getting a promotion at work, being able to lose weight, or buying a new car. Now make a second list of moments of where you felt gratified because you helped others achieve their goals. Maybe you supported someone who ran their first 5k. Perhaps you showed someone how to bring in another revenue stream that got them closer to getting a better place to live for their kids. Then compare the two lists. The goal is to have the one where helping others is longer than the list where self-gratification is the focus.

_____

_____

_____

_____

_____

_____

_____

_____

_____

"If you're going through, hell, keep going."

Winston Churchill

POWERFUL

Only YOU have the power to change your current circumstances, so stop blaming the world. Stop making excuses. Placing blame is a cop-out. Take the blame, don't place it! It's up to you to believe you can do more and guess what; YOU CAN! It happens the moment you realize it is no else's fault but yours.

Here's what I do know:

You have it in you to do great things! You have the power to touch so many lives, but you have to touch yours first. Every day you wake up you are setting an example for anyone that sees you. Whether it's your kids, family, friends, coworkers, or anyone that crosses your path, you are setting the bar, so I'm urging you to raise it up.

Stop noticing the negative and start promoting the positive. Train your mind to do more. Believe in more and simply be thankful for every additional day we get to wake up and truly live.

Live as if there's no tomorrow. Love so strongly that the ones you love will never feel anything greater than the way you feel towards them. Work hard knowing nothing comes easy. Show the world that through faith and the right mindset you can accomplish anything.

Teach the world to see the good in their lives and to realize all the "trying times" aren't going to go away. You have to embrace them and expect them, but don't dwell on them. Fight through them and make yourself stronger, learning from them every day. You have greatness in you! It's time to take responsibility and show the world what you're made of.

Let's do this:

Identify a time when you know you did not give it your all, when you didn't believe, or you were too complacent. Call yourself out on every bit of mediocrity you allowed yourself to walk in. What were you thinking? How were you feeling? Why do you think you allowed yourself to be in that place?

Once you see it all in front of you, begin to write affirmations that you can recite daily, use to pull that greatness out of you, and use to keep you focused on your goals.

For example, maybe you allowed yourself to give up on your fitness goals. You told everyone you were going to the gym, but slowly you crept back into a life of sitting in front of the sofa eating pizza because it was "too hard." Your affirmation may say, "I am committed to being healthy and fit." Now, do it.

_____

_____

_____

_____

_____

_____

_____

_____

_____

_____

_____

_____

_____

"The mystery of human existence lies not in just staying alive, but in finding something to live for."

Fyodor Dostoyevsky

PURPOSE

Ghandi once said, "The day the power of love overrules the love of power, the world will see peace." Purpose is defined as the reason for which something is done or created, or for which something exists. Have you ever wondered what your purpose is? Do you ever feel you're meant to do more? Are you doing what you're truly passionate about? Do you feel fulfilled?

Look, these questions have many answers, but to have access to your full potential, you have to open up your mind and search for what your purpose in life is. Completely understanding the impact you can have on the lives of many can have a profound effect on the legacy you leave on this earth.

The first thing to do is answer these questions and no matter what your answer is, accept and embrace it. Be who you are! Don't change your goals based on the minds of the masses. Set the tone of your life and get to know you. Your desires and dreams are yours alone and are as important as those of the great achievers in this world. You need to know deep down, that what you have to say is powerful and will change the lives of many. One person can change the world; live by that fact! The question to ask yourself is if you have the courage to find your purpose?

Purpose moves people to rebuild and remake the world. When you have faith and believe in what you're going to accomplish, nothing will be able to hold you back. Your passion for your purpose needs to be bigger than the naysayer's commitment to bring you down.

Most people have heard the phrase "what's behind your why?" Why do you get up every day? Your purpose is a huge part of your why. You can't express great thought and sit back and not take action on that thought. You'll never be taken seriously when you procrastinate on what you know can impact the world in a positive way. When you sit and do nothing, you guarantee that.

You must allow your passion to become your purpose and watch how that passion for your purpose will soon become your profession. Your life has purpose. Your story has purpose. Your voice matters and can impact more people than you can possibly imagine. Don't be afraid to go out and be vulnerable in this world and share your gift. Be open to critics and be ready for the negativity. Block the bad out and concentrate on the goal at hand. You're not going to win everyone over, but if you touch one life, you win. There's an old saying, "Work for a cause, not for applause."

You're alive for a reason. If you feel your heart beating at this very moment, that's purpose. That's a higher being telling you there's a reason why you're still here. You have a job to do. Find out what it is and do everything within your power to make your presence known. Efforts and courage are great words, but they aren't anything without purpose and the direction of where you're going.

If you fall asleep with a dream, you should wake up with a purpose. Dreams become reality the moment your purpose gives you extraordinary vision to discover what you are truly capable of. Define your own purpose. It should be useful, honorable, compassionate, and most importantly, it should make a profound difference in the lives of many for years to come. Be bold enough to use your voice as a vehicle for those who may not be brave enough just yet.

If I'm being honest, people that say "Money won't make you happy," are wrong in one way, but right in another. Having money makes life easier and allows you multiple ways to accomplish great things in this world, but it doesn't guarantee to project your purpose. When you can pay your bills on time and not have to worry about obligations or the daily fight to provide, you have a peace of mind in an area where most struggle to survive.

That being said, having money doesn't always mean life's easier or better. The greatest tragedy in the world is a person with the income potential and power to change the world, but has that lack of passion to do so. Living a life without purpose, isn't living at all. There's a quote by Mark Twain that reads, "The two most important days in your life are the day you are born and the day you find out why."

The impact this one quote will have on the lives of those for generations to come is amazing. Years ago, Mark Twain decided his voice had to be heard. He thought of many great things to say and hoped that one day people would remember him as the person who inspired others to have purpose in who they are and what they can accomplish. With a few words he did just that, and you can too. The minute you follow what you're sincerely passionate about is the moment you will find your purpose.

Here's what I do know:

If you pay attention to the things you are naturally drawn to or feel emotionally connected to, you will undoubtedly find your path, passion, and purpose in life. You must be brave enough to just follow your heart. We live our lives by following the decisions of others rather than having the faith in who we are, and in what touches our soul.

You have to realize that your life is yours alone! Only you can decide to let the world know who you are.

Do yourself and the world a favor and announce yourself. Don't allow anything to get in the way of the message you need to give. You must live your life to the fullest. Will Smith said, "You don't have to be fearless, but don't let fear stop you from doing what you're meant to be great at."

You have your own unique gift, special talent, or a blend of both, to share with the world. In his speeches, Les Brown often quotes Miles Monroe who said, "The graveyard is the richest place on earth, because it is here that you will find all the hopes and dreams that were never fulfilled, the books that were never written, the songs never sung, the inventions never shared, the cures never discovered, all because someone was too afraid to take that first step to carry out their dream."

I guess the only question is once you find your purpose and your passion, are you willing to go after it? I don't know much, but I do know that life is too short not to share your gift with the world. Don't let what you have to offer us all end up in a graveyard of undiscovered dreams. The time for you is now!

Let's do this:

Identify your passion. What is the thing you dream about and think about all the time? If all your bills were paid and all you had to do was wake up and do what you loved, what would that be? Who would it help? How would it look? Make a list of at least 3 things. Then find the common thread that ties them all together. That is your purpose. Identify any obstacles that may be stopping you from living it. Then crush them one by one.

_____

_____

_____

_____

_____

_____

_____

_____

_____

_____

_____

_____

_____

_____

_____

"It is not what you are that hold you back. It is what you think you are not."

Unknown

SELF-ESTEEM

Self-esteem is defined as confidence in one's own worth or abilities; self-respect. A feeling of satisfaction that someone has in himself or herself and his or her own abilities. All too often we find ourselves questioning choices we make, the path we choose, the decisions that will ultimately control our future. We don't allow the benefits of what we have to offer to actually come to fruition.

Positive self-esteem is how we think others see our value to the world. This is not to be confused with arrogance or being cocky, but exuding positive value through the energy we give off. Low self-esteem comes from individuals not being able to realize their full potential. They feel as if they are inferior or don't have what it takes to do great things. This inevitably affects our business life, personal relationships, and our future projected value to the world.

Here's a fact, when you're crushing life and are on top of the world, it's easy to go through life with a shining light over your head. You have confidence, a good sense of personal limitations, ability to solve problems, make mistakes and learn from them, know where you're going, set goals others seem to think are unreachable, are completely optimistic, have good self-direction, understand and are comfortable with your emotions and why they're happening when they are, and most importantly, have an ability to trust others.

When you have self-confidence and a higher self-esteem, you are not afraid to trust the process and the people in it. You expect hiccups and know you'll be ready to handle them. When you have lower self-esteem, the word trust, doesn't usually exist in your vocabulary. Everyone is out to get you and no one cares about your worth or what you may or may not be able to accomplish in your life.

Here's what I do know:

I know that individuals with positive self-esteem usually have some sort of daily routine to help keep them on the right path. This could be listening to motivational speeches on the way to work, listening to audio books, using your car as a mobile college, creating a vision board of goals and measure daily how close they are, writing down goals at night and getting up the following day to review them, and forming a step-by-step process to obtain such goals. Individuals with positive self-esteem do things like forcing themselves to work out in the morning while writing something positive on social media, in a journal or on a blog, to get their mind right and guarantee a positive start to every day. What you do in the first 20 minutes of your day sets the tone for your entire day.

These routines keep their mind in a constant state of positivity. They expect bad things to happen, but aren't allowing those things to control their day. They don't say things like, "Why me?" "It never ends!" "I can't catch a break." "I can't win!" Instead, they choose to take situations head on and solve each issue at hand, turning each trying time into an opportunity to grow.

These individuals see the value in everything. They see the positive in everything, not allowing any tough moment, no matter how miniscule or how gigantic, to alter the path of their future. These powerful individuals don't allow any negativity from anyone or anything remotely close to their circle.

I also know that individuals with low self-esteem constantly question their judgement. They don't allow themselves to win. They don't give themselves a chance to grow, and most of the time take the path of least resistance in order to just get by. They don't have the confidence to see a better tomorrow, even though the strength inside is more powerful than they can ever imagine. They usually place blame on others, rather than accepting their current circumstances being solely because of the choices they've made.

If you're not careful, low self-esteem can build up over a lifetime, and become ingrained in your feelings and emotions, forcing you down the road to depression. We must recognize the small things before they escalate to a larger thing that may take over our mind, body, and soul. Usually you'll hear things like, "I can't do that," or "I don't know if I can do that," or "I don't think I can do this job." When the positive self-esteem individuals will say, "I can do that and if I can't right now, I will shortly," or "I never question my ability to do anything because I know I have it in me," or "I can do this job. I will do whatever it takes to guarantee my success."

The differences between the two are huge when it comes to the ability to overcome, thrive, or guarantee a successful future. You must be able to see yourself there. Truly see yourself winning and doing things others won't because you feel what you have to offer this world is on a level not yet recognized. You must have faith in yourself and what you're capable of before you can go after the things you're trying to accomplish.

Try saying things like:

· I will fail, and I will fail again, but I will fail better!

· I have what it takes.

· I will learn from every trying time.

· I respect myself and what I can do.

· I feel great.

· Life is good, and I'm going to make it better.

· I care about myself.

· I applaud others who win.

· I help others.

· I won't ever give up.

· I will always give it my all.

Listen, it's easy when you are on top, but it's not so easy when you're not. We all have to start from somewhere, and that somewhere is different for everyone. If I'm as honest as I can be, the moment you begin to blame anyone other than yourself for your current circumstances is the day you lose. You will never grow. You will never learn. You will never respect your path. You usually make excuses as to why others are winning. You secretly hate when others are doing better than you. I mean, I could go on and on, but the truth is, life's too short! All the time you're wasting on excuses could be applied and used as positive energy to guarantee a better tomorrow.

Look, I'm not 6 feet tall, dark skin, with a six-pack, so, what do I do? Do I make statements like "that person is just lucky?" Not at all. See the value in who you are. Find out what's unique about you and don't be afraid to be different. See the beauty you have to offer this world just the way you are. Don't question why you don't look or act like someone else, instead be you! You're more than good enough. You are great! You are exceptional! However, you're only all these great things if you see yourself as these things. How you view yourself will ultimately set the rhythm of your future in motion. It's up to you to decide how it plays out.

I know this, the day I realized I wasn't like anyone else but myself, and I finally saw the value in what I had to offer the world, that was the day my life began. I let nothing bring me down. I didn't listen to any negativity. My circle became smaller and smaller, but my integrity and faith in what I'm on this earth to do became bigger than ever.

I humbled myself, not allowing any portion of ego to get in the way of my future, and I realized that lessons learned are better than money earned. Money will follow a great mind, but without massive action and believing in your opportunity to seize every moment, you will never realize your full potential.

I'm not asking you, I'm telling you right here and now to scream at the top of your lungs,

"Enough is enough! I am great! I am powerful! I will succeed! I respect the person I am! I am going to win! Nothing can stop me! I'm beautiful in my own way! I will do things others won't! My life is good, but I'm just getting started!"

Let's be clear, this process can start at any age or any time in your life. I've seen 65-year-old individuals start successful, multi-million dollar businesses because it took them that long to finally believe they could!

You're going to fall. You're going to go through some extremely tough times. You're going to think you're at rock bottom at times, but it is your ability and belief that nothing can hold you down and you're one step away from getting right back up. Be powerful, people! Embrace all that life has to offer; the good and the bad. Be bold in your attempt at greatness. Have faith and respect for who you are and deep down know that you deserve to win. I don't know much, but I know you can do this and more. It's time!

Let's do this:

Reflect on a time when you let low self-esteem rob you of an opportunity at greatness. Did you want to start a new business, write a book, or maybe enter a professional relationship and didn't. Now that you have identified that time, pay attention to all the pieces that fueled that low self-esteem. Did you tell yourself you couldn't? Were you comparing yourself to someone else and their success?

Did you quit before you got started because you thought it was going to be too hard.

Be real with yourself. Now take the time to call out all that stuff that held you back. Write out every negative thought you had. Put down all the destructive things you said. Once you have everything down, use this as a way for you to be accountable to yourself. If you begin to think thoughts or say things that are on this list, you know you are not in the right mindset to win. Stop it and do better.

_____

_____

_____

_____

_____

_____

_____

_____

_____

_____

_____

_____

_____

"If you are working on something exciting that you really care about, you don't have to be pushed. The vision pulls you."

Steve Jobs

VISION

Understanding your vision: The hard truth is that most have an "idea" of what they want out of life, but very few have a "vision." When you have an idea, you are just thinking of what could be. When you have a vision, you're going after what should be.

Here's what I do know:

The average person never follows through with an idea. For instance, how someone says something is just as important as how they live it. If you say to yourself, "I would like to write a book," rather than saying "I am going to write a book," you set yourself up two different ways. In one way, you're simply asking your subconscious if you should or should not. On the other hand, you're literally telling yourself that you're going to write the book. Yet, neither of these normally get the job done alone unless you add the steps of writing down your goals, putting a plan together to reach your goals, and committing action to your words.

When you have a vision, it is imperative that you are clear on the choices you're going to have to make to accomplish what you're setting out to do. You have to understand that there will be sacrifices made for you to achieve your goals. You have the time, but what are you going to do to manage it accordingly to guarantee you exceed what your potential worth is?

Finding your vision can sometimes be harder than you think, but I'm going to tell you a way to know what it is instantly. Here's what I want you to do. Think of anything you've ever wanted to do and finally take action and get it done. Even if it's trying it one time, DO IT! You have to give yourself the opportunity to see what that moment feels like. You have to push the limits of what you think you may or may not be capable of in order to find what makes you tick.

This process will force you into having a feeling of fulfillment when you do that one thing that makes you feel powerful, empowered, and humble. When this happens, you start believing in yourself more. Your wealth starts being realized in value rather than dollar bills. You will feel your purpose is bigger than ever before. You become inspired not only by those around you, but by reaching heights you've only dreamt of reaching. At this moment, you start to actually believe in your vision.

The game plan does have to be set up properly though. Don't just jump into something and think that's what you're meant to do. You have to try the things you've been afraid of trying in order to find what completes you as a person. Jobs and careers come and go, but your calling, your mission in life, your value added to the world is the legacy you will leave that will define, and be a reflection of who you are and who you were. Your impact on the world won't be left here by your awards at work. Your impact on this earth will be left by the lives you touch.

Personal vision to me is the clear mental image of a preferable future brought in part, only by the realization of what not only could be but what will be brought to fruition through self-growth and circumstances. Make sure your vision adds massive value to your life and the lives others.

Vision is about developing clarity and purpose around the largest and most life-changing goals you have.

Once you find your vision, you have to know things aren't always going to be perfect. Good things are going to happen, but you must be prepared for the bad as well. Your circumstances will be defined by the road you choose once options are available. If something bad happens, you can choose to give up, slow down, question your role in life, lose self-confidence, blame it on others, allow excuses to take over your mind or simply believe that what you're trying to achieve is just not possible anymore. On the other hand, if you decide to find the positive in every negative and be ready knowing these difficult times are coming, then you've found the cure to your soul.

When something challenging happens in your life, you either give up or get up. Instead of falling to the needs of insecurity and self-doubt, how about controlling your future by believing in yourself even more? You can choose to fight back, keep going, never even think about giving up and gain more confidence in your ability to handle anything that comes your way. Instead of placing blame, you can start accepting it. Start to work on yourself and give credit to what you know you can do if you just stay the course. When you finally take control, expecting tough times to come, you'll stop making excuses, and you'll start to create solutions.

Your self-value through the vision you have, and utilizing your God-given talent to find the greatness within you, will soon be an infectious energy for the world to see. Then, and only then, will you know your true potential.

Never try to be someone you're not. The world has too many individuals trying to create an image, rather than realizing the gift in just being real. We are falling behind because our role models are just twisted productions of someone they thought they should be, rather than taking hold of what they have to offer to the world and being authentic. If I can give you one crucial piece of advice while reading this book, it would be this:

Be authentic in every way.

Don't be a byproduct of what someone else is. The world is lacking real these days. There is no other you. The moment you own that is the day you will start to visualize your future.

Let's do this:

Write down all the things you think might lead you to your vision. This may include things you've done that you'd like to do again. Most importantly, write down things you haven't done yet that you know will add value to your life and help you find out what your aspirations and goals are. Once you've done this, write down the reason why you'd like to do each of these things and how it will impact your life and possibly the lives around you in a positive way.

Now that you've done that, it's time to get the game plan to make sure all of this happens. Make a timeline for when you will complete each task and push yourselves. Put yourself in an uncomfortable situation. This will maximize your ability to get things done.

When you've completed each task, find out which one impacted your life the most or made you feel like you wanted more. Believe me, you'll know when it happens. You shouldn't move on until you've made your list and completely understand your vision or at least your journey of finding your vision. Today is the day you chose to change your life forever. Enjoy it!

_____
_____
_____
_____
_____
_____
_____
_____
_____
_____
_____
_____
_____
_____
_____

"Desire, burning desire, is basic to achieving anything beyond ordinary."

Joseph B. Wirthlin

DESIRE

Desire is defined as a strong feeling of wanting to have something or wishing for something to happen. You have to have desire. You can't even begin to start your life without the desire for something more. Having desire usually comes from a place of wanting recognition coupled with your accomplishments. It's not necessarily about what we desire as much as it is about being known for your great feats. When you want something bad enough, it will light a fire within you, igniting more drive than you've ever had before.

When you want something bad enough, you will do anything it takes to get it. You don't question your choice, you just do what it takes to make it happen. The obstacles that you see become minuscule and your mind is programmed to believe in what you know you can accomplish.

Look, what if I told you tomorrow that I had a bag full of money that would change your life forever, and you'd never have to worry about anything ever again, as long as you completed that one task I'm asking of you. How fast do you think you'd find a way to get it done?

Life is about the choices and decisions you make to complete the need for what you desire. You can't go through life not seeking more, wanting more and just accepting the fact that you are what you are. You have to set goals and allow yourself the opportunity to grow.

This is exactly the reason people have vision boards. They make a list of their desires. They visualize them and they set a plan of action on how to obtain each of them. There's always a process, always some heartache and there are always different ways of achieving your goals as long as your belief in what you can accomplish is greater than your "what ifs." Don't question why you desire something. If you want it, you can achieve it. There is no science behind making it happen. It is literally about allowing yourself to be open to the possibility that you can and will be more.

Here's what I do know:

Most people get in their own way. They have a great idea, and at that very moment, their desire to make it happen is on fire. The only problem is 99.99999% of all individuals don't follow through the next day. They let time and lack of determination or fear stop them from doing something exceptional that could change their lives forever. It's sad really.

Have you ever asked yourself why you're afraid to go after what you desire most? Fear of failure? What will people think? Will they question your ability or your drive? Or maybe you feel not having money will stop you from making it happen? Let me tell you this, it's definitely easier to make money when you have money, but that never stopped any strong-willed person who truly went after what they desired most from becoming a game changer.

If you wanted it bad enough, you'd find the money if you're willing to put in the work, just like many before you. Ask yourself what's the reason you haven't done something great already? Can you think of one? You're going to find a reason, I promise you. Now, what if you used that same energy to find a solution?

Our society has done everything they can to teach people how to be the ultimate closers. Except the problem is most of the world closes themselves more than they do others. I want you to think of a time, right now, that you had a great idea and did nothing to make it happen, even though everything in your heart told you "this is the one." I bet you told your friends about it. I bet you went home and did a little research on it to see if there was anything out there like it. I bet that after not taking the massive action you needed to make it happen, you told the world how someone else "stole" your idea and now they're rich. Guess what people? That's on you! Your desire wasn't bigger than your "what ifs" man! You chose to give in, rather than go after what you thought you wanted most. The truth is, if you really wanted it, you would've made it happen.

Now I want you to think of something you wanted, and you made it happen. It could be buying a home, getting the job you've always wanted, buying that new car, going on a trip of a lifetime, or whatever it was, but you desired it so much that nothing got in your way of making it a reality. If you're thinking of it right now, ask yourself what you did differently that time? What action did you take? Did you believe you could make it happen? Did you find a solution, rather than excuses? How did you accomplish such a goal?

See there's a huge difference between just wanting something and truly desiring something. When you just want something, you talk about it. When you desire it, you'll do anything to make it happen. Desire can be something as simple as wanting to know what happened to that one friend you knew in high school 20 years ago. You'll end up finding out what happens to them because you know what steps to take or at least where to start to ensure your desire is met. The problem with a desire of something larger like buying a building, being famous, or going after something some see as "unrealistic," is that you don't know the steps to take to make it come to fruition.

We get scared. We question ourselves on whether that thing we desire can become a reality. Self-doubt sets in and people retreat. They don't stand strong. They simply give up on the idea, and this process of desire replays itself over and over again throughout their lives. This is guaranteed to cripple your mindset. It will happen so often that you eventually give up on accomplishing anything you feel is out of your reach.

You have to choose to change your mindset now! You cannot allow yourself to give up on yourself. You have one life to live, to give everything you have to make your dreams come true. If you go full force believing you can have anything you desire, you will eventually become unstoppable. Yes, failure will occur. Man, I've failed so many times I can't even count them all. But that goes with that old saying, "If at first, you don't succeed, try try again!"

Our world is so used to seeing all the rich and wellness in the extraordinary lives of others, that we seem to have a full disregard for the efforts of the success giants of the world. We conveniently forget about, or don't know about, the amount of times they failed, or the work they've put in to be exactly where they are now. They believed in themselves no matter what happened, no matter what anyone said, no matter how hard each day was, and no matter how many times they fell. Their desires weren't just goals to reach. They were changing lives, and were hell-bent on accomplishing this, and that's exactly what they did.

It's like a baby learning how to swim. People are shocked at their ability to swim at such a young age, but their desire to breathe was more significant than their desire to drown. When you want something that bad, you'll make sure it happens. The minute you want to succeed as bad as you want your heart to beat, nothing will get in the way of making it happen.

Find your desire; not just a goal and not just an idea. Find out what you truly want out of life. Find your reason to live and go after it. Don't settle. Don't worry about falling, just get back up and visualize your end goal. Allow yourself the chance to do more and believe in your ability to guarantee your desires become a reality. The only person stopping you is you.

Let's do this:

Write down one desire that you want more than anything.

_____

_____

Now, make a list of everything you think will stop you from achieving your goal.

_____

_____

_____

_____

Next, for each of the "excuses" you just wrote down, spend time finding a solution for each. If you don't know the solution, ask around or find one. I promise you, if you don't have the answer, someone else will.

_____

_____

_____

_____

_____

_____

_____

_____

_____

_____

Now, create your vision board of desires and set a game plan to start taking massive action to make it happen. With this, you will have your desire, your solutions, and your visualization. So, what's stopping you other than you? Good question, right?

"The moment you take responsibility for everything for your life, is the moment you can change anything in your life."

Hal Elrod

RESPONSIBILITY

Responsibility is defined as the state or fact of having a duty to deal with something or of having control over someone or yourself. Personal responsibility also means that when individuals fail to meet expected standards, they do not look around for some factor outside themselves to blame. We are all responsible for the different areas of our lives but many cannot consider ourselves for the blame of failure or lack of achievement due to our own actions. It's not that we don't view the process and learning, but we somehow find a reason why we didn't accomplish what we set out to do.

In today's society, we as strong-minded, strong-willed gladiators must fight for success. We have to realize that success comes from growth in understanding previous failures and applying those lessons. We have to search within ourselves to understand why the process isn't working and start to mend, prepare, or educate ourselves on our personal flaws or lack of knowledge on how the task at hand should be approached.

The top CEOs in the world read at least 3-5 hours a day, 60 books a year on average, and refuse to ever fall behind with any information pertaining to their field. This includes motivation, specific industry standards, how to lead, financial analyzation and more. At their level, the race to stay relevant is substantially higher than those starting out in their careers. You have to always be on top of your game.

The main differences between an industry giant and someone not as successful usually lies within the main frame of responsibility. They are constantly holding themselves accountable for their actions. This applies to their professional lives as well as their personal lives. Small, minute-by-minute decisions that can compound into larger ones can affect business growth and more. They don't allow themselves to fall short of what they could be, but when they do stumble, they don't place blame or waste energy finding an excuse of why they didn't succeed. They buck up and take responsibility.

Leaders in today's world search for their flaws or shortcomings. They love finding the weaknesses and transforming them into strengths. Taking responsibility for your life and actions is a sure way to realize the full potential in what you can be. You'll notice that most successful individuals realize they are far from perfect and when a mistake is made, they own up to it and educate themselves on what they could've done differently. They never stop searching for ways to grow and learn.

Taking responsibility should start at an early age. Responsibility can affect your entire life and mindset. You need to know that the energy wasted placing blame is energy wasted you could've used to find a solution. The destruction of personal responsibility occurs when people start to blame their family, their peers, their economic circumstances, or their society for their failure to meet standards. It's noticeably always everyone else around them rather than realizing it is specifically them.

More than ever, in today's society, individuals feel inferior when they feel as if they've failed. If they aren't top in their class, top of their field, top in sales, top in sports, and top in anything really, they feel a cold chill of lack of presence. This all stems from not being responsible for your current circumstances.

There are several areas where responsibility is essential in understanding your position, but some of the main ones the world focuses on today are education, marriage, and work. We can always find ways to shuck responsibility in these areas. An example of this is in education. By saying "I failed that test because they didn't give me enough time to study," is a copout. In marriage, pointing fingers rather than apologizing even when you swear you're in the right is a way of shucking or dodging responsibility as well. Is the risk worth more than the reward? Sometimes we have to take responsibility and be the bigger person just to end a fight or understand how the other may feel. In a work environment, there are so many to name, but one common example would be not hitting a goal, or exceeding company standards or over delivering where the company sees your exceptional value.

The strong in this day and age always understand where their limitations lie and then concentrate on turning a limitation into determination in excelling in that area of their lives. They don't question, find a reason to shuck responsibility, or dwell on the fact they aren't excelling in a specific area. Instead, they take all their energy and insert it into a place where accountability can be measured by effort. This process guarantees stability in growth. There's no chance of submission or giving in because they understand that the end goal is more important than their current face value as to how the world sees them at this very moment.

Here's what I do know:

There are two types of people in the responsibility world. You have the creator of growth person and the victim mentality person. The creator of growth person implies that every person willing to be more, understand their worth, their ability to be more and never, under any circumstances, place blame on anyone but themselves realizing that the wasted energy can be used more effectively to adhere to a bigger purpose or goal they seek. The victim mentality person is quick to place blame. These individuals find every reason outside of themselves for why a goal doesn't come to fruition. They spend more time talking about what could've been, rather than searching for the reason it is what it is. For instance, a salesperson has an opportunity for a sale but realizes the client is upset about something that had nothing to do with them. In a victim mentality, the salesperson is quick to place the blame as if the issues have nothing to do with them. The creator of growth person would respond in a much more compassionate and understanding role, taking the responsibility and trying to find a solution on how to fix the issue immediately.

Responsibility in any field is more important than most people think. It's a crucial part of your life as a whole. From a creator standpoint, these individuals are empowered. From a victim mindset, these individuals are powerless. A creator believes they have complete control of their future, where a victim believes that no matter what choices they make, their future is already set and nothing they do will change the outcome. A victim mentality is a sure way to minimize life's value quickly, without any chance of redeeming your full potential.

You must take full responsibility for everything in your life. You have to realize that no one is going to do it for you. No one is going to take your pain, fight your good fight or force growth for you, but everyone wants to yield the highest of results for less work. When you run from the true cause because the finger of certainty is pointing directly at you, you have no chance to reveal the power you have to change the world and utilize the specific gift you've been given.

You can change yourself. One of the biggest downfalls in today's world is that the masses feel entitled to a life of wealth and fame. They feel as if life's gifts are supposed to come jumping out at them. Like having a beautiful, healthy family, spending quality time with them, career opportunities just handed out, having the perfect marriage or relationship with your partner. These are things we all hope to have, but most have to work hard to get them and then maintaining them is another level of responsibility few these days are willing to take control of. Hence the lack of effort to saving marriages which has led to a higher divorce rate or how about keeping your job or fighting for what you know is right.

If you take anything at all away from this book, (although I hope you take more than this), if there's one thing I want you to get out of reading this, that one thing is that there is only one person responsible for the quality of life you live. That person is absolutely you!

You have to realize that society has been trained and conditioned to blame things on anyone other than themselves. To separate fault or failure from personal responsibility and find blame to place on people for things such as relationships with friends and family, economy evaluations, coworkers, your partner, lack of money or the obstacles of life in general from getting what they feel they're worthy of receiving. Let me be real right now, these are all excuses for individuals looking to retreat or escape from self-loathing. They think they are keeping themselves confident in their ability to excel, but in reality, they soon realize that little voice in their head (truth) starts to whisper words of wisdom verifying life lessons they soon will learn.

Use your life challenges as growth mechanisms to allow your mind to flourish in any field. Understand that your full potential will never be reached by playing the victim role. Your self-worth should mean more to you than that. You have a chance to truly grow, but the only real way to do that, is to be responsible for every circumstance in your life.

From this day forward, start realizing that no one is perfect; not you, not me, not anyone. You have a chance to make things right. The mediocre spend all their energy on things like always needing to be right, ignorance, lack of awareness or maybe just a need to feel safe limiting the reward by minimizing the risk of reducing self-value. I don't know everything, and I'm still growing myself every day, but these are the things about responsibility that I do know.

Let's do this:

Name three things about yourself you need to work on personally and business-wise. Think of one time when you were wrong, but refused to admit you were. Think of a situation where you may have played the victim role instead of gathering information from a creator's standpoint that could've resulted in increased self-awareness. Finally, grade yourself. Which one are you at this very moment, the "victim or creator," and write your reason why. Complete these exercises. You'll be shocked at the results and how much you teach yourself. You know who you are; sometimes it's just writing it down and reading it back that makes it more real.

_____

_____

_____

_____

_____

_____

_____

_____

_____

_____

_____

_____

_____

_____

_____

"Never underestimate your own strength. You were born with a purpose and are blessed with the power to achieve it."

Leon Brown

UNDERESTIMATE

Underestimate is defined as the estimation of something to be smaller or less important than it actually is. Studies, for years, have shown that high achievers underestimate their talents, while underachievers overestimate theirs.

At face value, underachievers are sometimes cocky or arrogant, and it may seem as if they have full control over their mindset. Many people that think this way overestimate what they can achieve or take little or no action in following through with what they say they will accomplish. They have a fire burning inside of them to do more, which is a great thing, but they question the process. Usually these individuals, deep down, believe there's an ability they have to share with the world and truth be told, there is.

The hard truth is that they're usually too afraid to let their fears be known. This limits their ability to grow, allowing ego to stand in the way of what they could be.

On the other side, there are your success giants. Your overachievers. These types of individuals believe there's always something new to learn. They understand and believe in the process. They also set goals and accomplish them, but also feel as if there's always room for improvement.

They believe anything can be accomplished, but one of the main reasons for their ability to thrive is they don't even know how great they are. This keeps a torch within them burning daily, pushing for superstardom. Mostly they underestimate what they feel they can accomplish and this questionable thought process, yields them massive results because they're always going to find out if they're truly capable of pushing the limits more and more every day.

Some underestimate even the power of a touch, a compliment, a smile, a sense of caring or just listening to someone who wants to be heard. It's not always about personal growth. We sometimes underestimate the things we see as minuscule, not realizing the massive effect it may have on the lives we're fortunate enough to come into contact with daily.

Personally, I feel everyone has a gift. You just have to find out what it is and do all you can to share it with the world. So, if you're one of those people who sincerely believe you have something powerful to share, don't underestimate it, have faith in it! If you believe, others will too. You can't underestimate positive power; you just can't. There are so many powerful people and extraordinary gifts wasted due to lack of confidence or underestimating their ability to be more that it really is a shame.

It's easy to look at the rich and famous and feel as if they're different than you. Or feel that there's something inside of them that you don't have. A lot of people even feel as if they don't have much to give to the world, or have much to offer others. When you start to feel this way, your limitations become limitless. You never truly believe in what you can or will accomplish. You start to find reasons not to do something rather than finding solutions of why you should.

If you studied the powerful minds of our existence and asked them when their turning point was, you'd find a similar response from each one stating that the most important, life-changing move they've ever made was allowing their mindset never to underestimate what they could accomplish while being humble and realizing there's always more to learn. This combination of thinking is a recipe for maximum growth.

Here's what I do know:

The power of optimism begins to flow through your veins the minute you recognize your gift and become passionate about sharing it with the world, never underestimating the lives you will touch. I'm here to tell you, you can and will change lives. You will be great! You will accomplish all your goals. You will help others reach things they've once thought unreachable, but it all starts with believing in you first.

Don't rob yourself of any opportunity by underestimating who you are and what you're made of. Let yesterday be yesterday and prove to yourself today that you're more than you thought. Embrace it. Very few realize their gift and use it to its full potential, and you have the power to be a part of those few.

It's fine when others underestimate you. Usually, this means they're scared of what you may accomplish due to their lack of belief on what they can accomplish. Do me a favor though, don't ever underestimate your ability to do exactly what you know you can. Understanding and having an optimistic state of mind will guarantee that you recognize where your areas of growth are and where you need to spend time focusing on so that you can be more than you are today! The only way to succeed is to believe you can! You have greatness in you and you can't allow any limitation to cloud your judgment on reaching your full potential in life.

Don't underestimate yourself, your environment, your co-workers, your competition, your gift or your ability to touch lives positively. You have one life to live, and you're not allowed to go backwards. I won't let you! Yes, you're going to fall, as we all do, but don't allow lack of judgment or belief in what you can be stop you from getting up and sharing your gift with the world.

The choice is yours to make right now. Do you truly believe in yourself? Do you know you have a gift? Do you want to live your life questioning what you could've been? Do you want to live in a mediocre state of mind? Do you want to live unwealthy? And what I mean by unwealthy is, in love, life, laughter and happiness in knowing you're doing all you can to leave a legacy of powerful information to live and help change lives long after you're gone.

Be all of you, always! Give 100% of the person you are and the person you can be! Effort lies in the ability to understand fully what you can accomplish! That's more than good enough, I promise.

Let's do this:

Take some time to reflect on when you underestimated yourself. You thought you couldn't do it so you didn't even try. What was that opportunity missed? It is important for you to identify it, because you still have a chance to succeed. Whether it is personally or professionally, as long as you have life, you have an opportunity to work to achieve your goals. Go and get it!

_____

_____

_____

_____

_____

_____

_____

_____

_____

_____

_____

_____

_____

_____

_____

_____

Made in the USA
Las Vegas, NV
29 April 2021